One Wolf
HOWLS

by Scotti Cohn   illustrated by Susan Detwiler

Publisher's Cataloging-In-Publication Data

Cohn, Scotti.

One wolf howls / by Scotti Cohn ; illustrated by Susan Detwiler.

p. : col. ill. ; cm.

Summary: The months of the year and the numbers 1 through 12 are used in rhyming text to introduce children to the behavior of wolves in natural settings. Includes "For Creative Minds" educational section.

Interest age level: 004-008.
Interest grade level: P-3.

ISBN: 978-1-934359-92-1 (hardcover)
ISBN: 978-1-607180-37-1 (pbk.)
ISBN: 978-1-607180-57-9 (eBook)
ISBN: 978-1-607180-47-0 (Spanish eBook)

QL737.C22 C64 2009
599.773   2008936038

Printed in China

Sylvan Dell Publishing
976 Houston Northcutt Blvd., Suite 3
Mt. Pleasant, SC 29464

Thanks to the staff at both the Wolf Park and the International Wolf Sanctuary and to Gina Schrader, Conservation Associate at Defenders of Wildlife, for verifying the accuracy of the information in this book. A special thanks to photographer Monty Sloan for providing the author photo, taken at Wolf Park in Battle Ground, Indiana.

One wolf howls in the January moonlight—
night light, dim light, midnight sky.
One wolf howls in the January moonlight
deep in the woods where the moon hangs high.

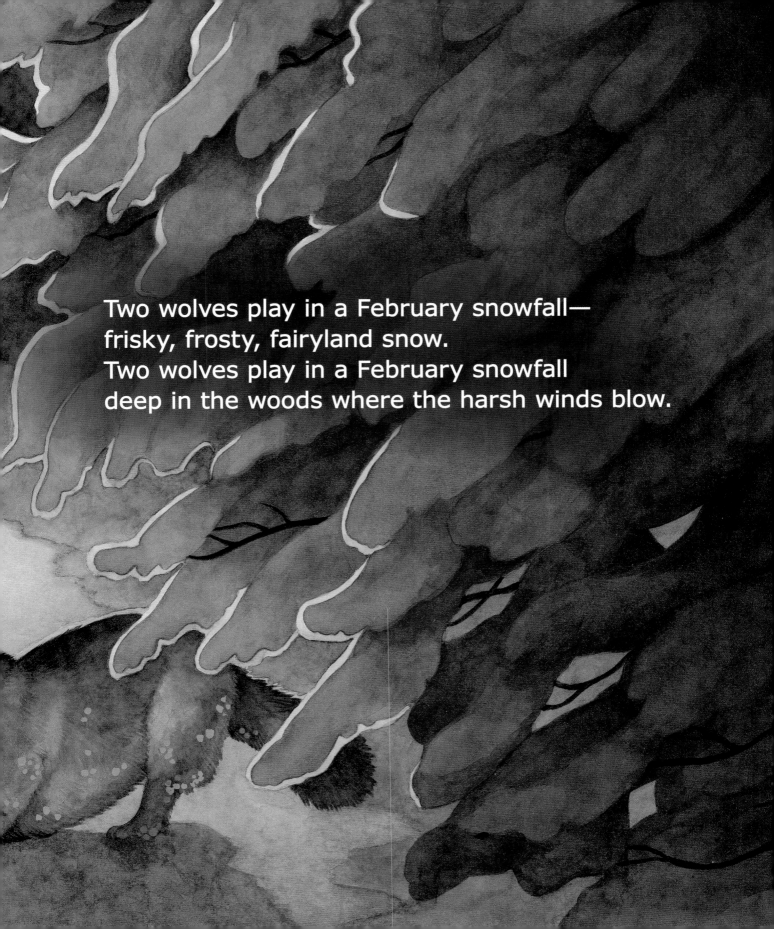

Two wolves play in a February snowfall—
frisky, frosty, fairyland snow.
Two wolves play in a February snowfall
deep in the woods where the harsh winds blow.

Three wolves bark on a brisk March morning—
danger, danger, humans in sight!
Three wolves bark on a brisk March morning
deep in the woods in the dawn's gray light.

Four wolves hunt in an April rainfall—
raindrops, rain drips, storm winds blow.
Four wolves hunt in an April rainfall
deep in the woods where the tall trees grow.

Five wolves peek at a bright May sunbeam—
fuzzy pups, funny pups, sniff and stare.
Five wolves peek at a bright May sunbeam
deep in the woods in the fresh spring air.

Six wolves nap in a warm June meadow—
snuffling, snorting, lost in their dreams.
Six wolves nap in a warm June meadow
deep in the woods by the bubbling streams.

Seven wolves trot through July's green grasses—
heads up, ears keen, paws keeping beat.
Seven wolves trot through July's green grasses
deep in the woods in the summertime heat.

Eight wolves dance in the August twilight—
splash feet, paddle feet, prance by the lake.
Eight wolves dance in the August twilight
deep in the woods as the owls awake.

Nine wolves hide on September hilltops—
shy ones, sly ones, no one sees.
Nine wolves hide on September hilltops
deep in the woods in the falling leaves.

Ten wolves sniff at October hoofprints—
tracking, chasing moose on the run.
Ten wolves sniff at October hoofprints
deep in the woods when the day is done.

Eleven wolves sleep in November shadows—
huddled up, cuddled up, snug and warm.
Eleven wolves sleep in November shadows
deep in the woods where they fear no harm.

Twelve wolves sing a December chorus—
howling, yowling with all their might.
Twelve wolves sing a December chorus
deep in the woods on a winter's night.

For Creative Minds

Wolf Communications Matching Activity

Match the communication description to the sketch showing the communication method. Answers are sideways on the next page. *Have you ever seen a dog use any of these communication methods?*

1. Wolves howl to:
   - Let others know where they are
   - Let others know that a hunt is about to start
   - Gather at the end of the hunt
   - Mark their territory for other wolves
   - Express fear
   - And, last but not least, because they like to

2. Alpha wolves will look other wolves directly in the eyes as a sign of dominance. Submissive wolves will not make eye contact.

3. Crouching down, slinking, or being on its back shows a wolf's submission.

4. The front bowed down and the back end up with a wagging tail is an invitation to play.

5. Dominant wolves hold their tails high—almost as though they are pointing at the sky.

6. Tails pointed down or between their legs show fear or submission.

7. Tails pointed straight out show interest or an attack.

8. Ears flat against the head show fear or submission.

9. Ears that are up show dominance, or that a wolf is listening or paying attention to something.

10. Ears pointed straight up and bared teeth show anger.

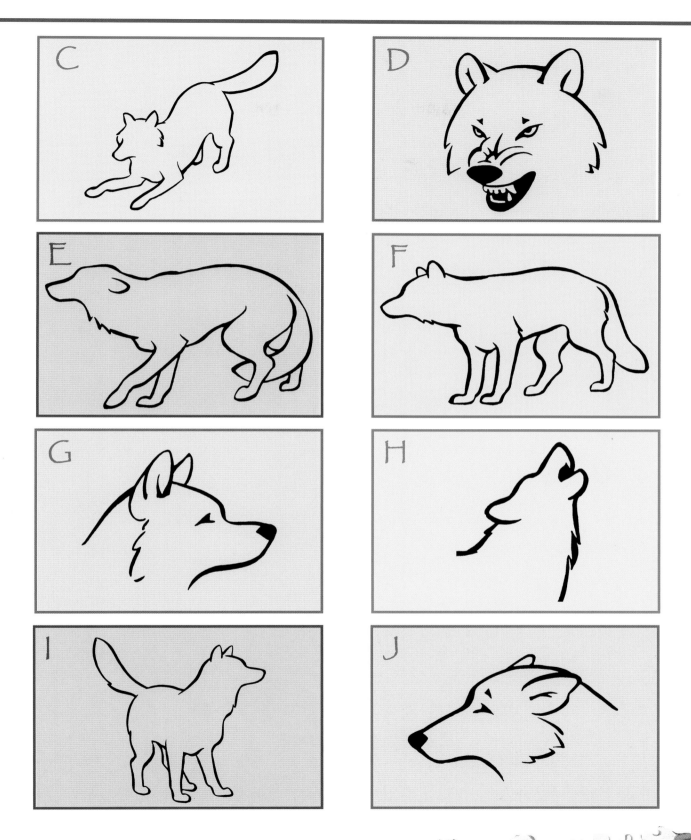

Wolf Fun Facts

Wolves are related to dogs — they are both canines. You might think of them as being distant cousins. Just like there are different types of dogs (poodles, labs, etc.), there are two main types of wolves: gray wolves (*Canis lupus*) and red wolves (*Canis rufus*). Some scientists are debating whether a third type, the Ethiopian wolf (*Canis simensis*), is a wolf or a jackal.

Wolves live in groups called packs. Each pack has an alpha, or leader, male and female. The size of a pack can range from just two to some Canadian or Alaskan packs having over 30 wolves! Most packs have between five and eight wolves. Larger packs have several females with pups.

Packs are territorial and will guard their territory against other wolves. The size of the territory depends on the season, the pack size and how much food is available. More food means smaller territory and less food means a larger territory. *Why do you think this is?*

Wolf Life Cycle

- Wolves are born in the spring, usually around April or May, when food is plentiful.

- A pair of gray wolves usually has an average of 6-7 pups, while red wolves have 3-5 pups.

- Pups weigh about 1 lb. (0.45 kg) when they are born.

- Like us, wolves are mammals. The pups drink their mother's milk for the first five weeks.

- For the next two weeks, they eat regurgitated food that other members of the pack bring back to them. Then they are able to eat solid food.

- The pups stay in the den until they are about eight weeks old.

- At seven or eight months, pups are almost full grown and start traveling with the pack.

- A fully grown wolf may leave its pack at age one or two to find a mate and start another pack.

- A female wolf starts having babies when she is about two years old.

- Adult gray wolves generally live 10 or 12 years. Red wolves generally live eight or nine years.

Wolf Calendar Activity

Assuming that the wolf pups were born on April 15, use the calendars and the information on the previous page to answer the questions. Answers are upside down below.

April

Sunday	Monday	Tuesday	Wednesday	Thursday	Friday	Saturday
	1	2	3	4	5	6
7	8	9	10	11	12	13
14	15	16	17	18	19	20
21	22	23	24	25	26	27
28	29	30				

1. On what day of the week were the wolf pups born?

2. Around what date did the pups eat their first regurgitated food?

May

Sunday	Monday	Tuesday	Wednesday	Thursday	Friday	Saturday
			1	2	3	4
5	6	7	8	9	10	11
12	13	14	15	16	17	18
19	20	21	22	23	24	25
26	27	28	29	30	31	

3. If they ate their first solid food two weeks later, what would be the date?

4. If they left the den when they were eight weeks old, what would the date be?

June

Sunday	Monday	Tuesday	Wednesday	Thursday	Friday	Saturday
						1
2	3	4	5	6	7	8
9	10	11	12	13	14	15
16	17	18	19	20	21	22
23 / 30	24	25	26	27	28	29

Looking at the illustrations, can you identify the seasons?

Answers: 1. Monday; 2. Around May 20th, 3. Around June 3rd, 4. Around June 10th

Hunting

Wolves are carnivores (meat eaters). Gray wolves like to eat large animals including elk, deer, moose, bison, caribou, and smaller animals like beavers. The smaller red wolves eat a combination of white-tailed deer, rabbits, raccoons and rodents.

They only hunt and eat what they need to survive and will often go for days without eating. Although wolves normally eat all of their kill, any food that is left is eaten by other animals like vultures, foxes, bears, coyotes, wolverines, or eagles.

When hunting, wolves can travel up to 25 or 30 miles (40 or 48 km) a day. They usually walk about 5 miles (8 km) per hour but can run as fast as 40 miles (64 km) per hour if chasing something.

When hunting, wolves generally attack the slower, older, or injured animals from herds. This helps to keep the herd of prey strong.

Endangered Wolves

Before European settlers arrived in North America, wolves roamed throughout the continent. However, settlers misunderstood and feared wolves and killed them. In fact, many states paid people a bounty (money) when they killed a wolf. Due to the widespread hunting and loss of habitat from settlers moving onto their land, wolves were in danger of disappearing from the face of the earth (endangered).

With fewer wolves, other animals, such as elk, started to graze in newly safe areas. But they overate in these areas, causing a loss of natural habitat for other, smaller animals.

Humans started to realize how important wolves were for maintaining the natural balance in a habitat and began protecting them under the law. In the northern Rockies, the Southwest, and North Carolina, wolves have been re-introduced into their native territories. In the Great Lakes region, they returned to the wild on their own.